For the Love of Music

The Remarkable Story of Maria Anna Mozart

by

Elizabeth Rusch

Paintings by

Steve Johnson and Lou Fancher

TRICYCLE PRESS

Berkeley

A Note on Language

Throughout the book, keyboard instruments are referred to as pianos. Maria and Wolfgang Mozart played clavichords, harpsichords, and fortepianos, precursors to the pianos we know today.

Many Mozart scholars refer to Wolfgang's sister as Nannerl to prevent confusion with her mother, who shared her name. But Nannerl was a childhood nickname. Wolfgang's pet names were Wolferl or Wolfgangerl, but biographers refer to him as Wolfgang Amadeus Mozart. Out of respect for Maria Anna Mozart, the author chose to use her given name.

About the Sonata Form

More than any other kind of music, Maria Anna Mozart played sonatas. A sonata can be a composition for piano alone (a piano sonata) or for a different instrument with or without piano accompaniment (such as a violin sonata). Sonatas generally have three or four parts, called movements. The first movement, which usually has a fast tempo, is often in three sections, where musical themes are introduced, explored, and revisited. The first movement can have a miniending called a coda. The second movement is often slower. Some sonatas include a dancelike movement before the final one. In this book, Maria Anna Mozart's story is told in sonata form and also features other musical terms found in sonata compositions.

Text copyright © 2011 by Elizabeth Rusch
Illustrations copyright © 2011 by Steve Johnson and Lou Fancher

All rights reserved. Published in the United States by Tricycle Press, an imprint of Random House Children's Books,
a division of Random House, Inc., New York.
www.randomhouse.com/kids

Tricycle Press and the Tricycle Press colophon are registered trademarks of Random House, Inc.

Reproductions of original sheet music and letters from the Mozart family © Internationale Stiftung Mozarteum (ISM).

Translations from the Mozart family letters from Emily Anderson's *The Letters of Mozart and His Family*, 1938, Macmillan and Co., reproduced with the permission of Palgrave Macmillan.

Portrait of Maria Anna Mozart by unknown artist © Lebrecht Music & Arts.

Library of Congress Cataloging-in-Publication Data

Rusch, Elizabeth.
  For the love of music : the remarkable story of Maria Anna Mozart / by Elizabeth Rusch. — 1st ed.
    p. cm.
  1. Berchtold zu Sonnenburg, Maria Anna Mozart, Reichsfreiin von, 1751-1829—Juvenile literature. 2. Pianists—
Austria—Biography—Juvenile literature. I. Title.
  ML3930.B444R87 2011
  786.2092—dc22
  [B]
                              2009045489

ISBN 978-1-58246-326-1 (hardcover)
ISBN 978-1-58246-391-9 (Gibraltar lib. bdg.)

Printed in China

Design by Lou Fancher
Typeset in ITC Garamond Book Condensed and Phylis Initials D
The illustrations in this book were rendered in fabric, paper, and oil and acrylic on canvas.

1 2 3 4 5 6 – 16 15 14 13 12 11

First Edition

For Isabelle Anna Rusch, who is free to follow her heart.
—*E.R.*

For Carol and Len, and for Jan.
—*S.T. & L.F.*

Piano Sonata
(A composition for piano)

When Maria Anna Mozart was a child, her life thrummed with music. Court musicians trumpeted French horns, choruses tra-la-la'ed, and countless fingers skittered up and down scales.

"Oh, father," Maria pleaded, "please teach me to play!"
And so he did.

The First Movement

(Where musical themes are introduced)

Maria pressed the smooth keys, and notes fluttered out like a fountain, like raindrops on a puddle, like a warm wind. Whenever Maria practiced, her squirmy little brother would snuggle into the folds of her skirt.

As Maria's fingers raced across the keyboard, Wolfgang would become still. When she finally laid her hands in her lap, the notes rang on in their ears.

Then one day, Wolfgang reached his pudgy fingers toward the keys.

Allegro

(The fast tempo of the first movement)

Enchanting! Wonders of Nature! Child Geniuses! That's
what the newspapers called young Maria and Wolfgang.
By the time Maria was ten, the two of them were playing
recitals throughout Europe. Dukes and duchesses, kings
and queens, and emperors and empresses gathered in
grand halls to hear them perform.

"Wolferl," Maria whispered, "just look at the crowd!
So many elegant people! So many beautiful clothes!"

Wolfgang's creativity delighted everyone and, at twelve,
Maria was considered one of the best pianists in Europe.

Development
(Where the themes of the first movement are explored)

On the long carriage rides between cities, Maria and Wolfgang sang, practiced their French and Italian, and teased each other with nicknames.

Wolfgang poked his sister's nose: "Horse face!"

Maria flipped his name: "Gnagflow!"

When they couldn't stand to be stuck in the back of the carriage one minute longer, they entered their imaginary world, the Kingdom of Back.

"This kingdom and its inhabitants," Queen Maria declared, "are hereby endowed with everything that can make good and happy children."

"I request a canary to sing for me," cried King Wolfgang.

"The Queen requires new ribbons for her gown—and pudding!"

They both giggled as the carriage bumped and jostled them from city to city.

While in England, their father fell ill. "Hush," their mother told them. "You must be quiet."

"But can't we play?" they pleaded, sliding onto the piano bench.

"No, let him rest."

So the children huddled in a corner and made music in their minds. Wolfgang composed his first symphony and Maria wrote it down. "Remind me to give something good to the horn!" Wolfgang said. And she did.

The house was silent, but Maria and Wolfgang imagined a symphony that sounded like laughter, like whispering secrets in three languages, like children at a court dance.

Recapitulation

(Where the themes of the first movement are reviewed)

When the carriage finally clattered back into Salzburg a few years later, everyone exclaimed: "Oh, how you've grown!" and "How handsome you both are!" And Maria and Wolfgang played their instruments more beautifully than ever.

Coda

(An ending)

But when it was time for the next tour–to Italy, the musical center of the world–Wolfgang climbed into the back of the carriage alone.

Maria was left at home.

The Second Movement
(Often slower)

In Salzburg, Maria shopped with her mother, gathered herbs, and mended clothes. "I'm going to take Miss Pimpes for a walk," she called.

But for the love of music, Maria lingered in local churches to hear the booming organ. She performed in private concerts before family and friends. She even composed her own music, which Wolfgang greatly admired.

The Third Movement

(Dancelike)

When Wolfgang returned home, he wrote his very first piano duet to play with his big sister. "Let me see!" she said, grabbing the sheet music and hurrying to the piano.

Both parts of the duet were difficult.

At the piano, their arms entwined, Maria and Wolfgang were equals.

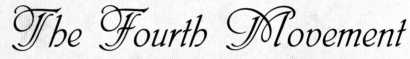

The Fourth Movement

(The final movement)

Memories of their travels washed over them.

"Remember when you climbed on the Empress's lap?" Maria said, laughing.

Wolfgang blushed. "I even gave her a kiss!"

"And all those pieces we played at the Archbishop's birthday? They were exquisite...."

Too soon, Wolfgang left again for another tour. Maria sobbed so hard, she got sick.

Sfzorando
(With emphasis)

But for the love of music, Maria kept playing. "Father, bring me more fugues from the Cathedral," she begged. And her playing became even more brilliant.

Ritardando
(To slow down)

Maria eventually married and moved to a tiny town far from her musical life in Salzburg. She brought a piano with her, and though she was busy with her five stepchildren, she made time to play every afternoon.

Fermata

(In which everything stops)

But during the first icy winters on the lake, her piano warped. Keys stuck and strings went out of tune. Still, for the love of music, Maria played on.

Cadenza

(A passage for a soloist to improvise)

When her children were born, concertos celebrated with her. When Wolfgang died so young, mournful masses cried with her. When Maria longed for her life in Salzburg, sonatas raised her from the tiny village to the very heavens.

Finale

(The last piece of music in a concert)

After her husband died, Maria returned to Salzburg. She practiced with court musicians, performed in private concerts, and taught promising young pianists.

One day, Maria received a special visitor—Wolfgang's son. "I see Wolferl in you," she said, laying a hand on his shoulder.

Maria led the young man to the piano of her childhood, the one she and her brother had played for countless hours.

Maria's nephew reached for the smooth keys.

The tone of the piano was soft, the notes rich. Maria was transported to the courts of Europe, where she'd performed for kings and queens, where she'd played duets with her brother, their arms entwined.

Maria sat beside her nephew. Together, she and Wolfgang's son played and played, for the love of music.

Encore: The Mystery of Maria Anna Mozart

At the stroke of midnight between July 30 and 31, 1751, in an apartment above a grocery in Salzburg, Austria, Maria Anna Walburga Ignatia Mozart was born. Daughter of court musician Leopold Mozart, Maria Anna was named after her mother, and as the first surviving child was considered a "stolen joy" by both. Five years later, in the same house, her only sibling, Wolfgang was born.

The Mozart family wrote many letters but most of Maria's have been lost, so much of her life is shrouded in mystery. What we do know is gleaned from letters written by Wolfgang and his parents and from news reports and diary entries of the time.

Music filled the Mozart household, with violinists, oboists, and singers practicing and giving impromptu concerts. It was Maria, though, who was Wolfgang's earliest inspiration. We know that when she was eight and he was three, he listened in awe as she practiced for hours each day. Wolfgang's first compositions were written in Maria's music book, which she kept her entire life.

In 1762 at age eleven, Maria set off on a musical tour with her brother Wolfgang, age six, and both parents. Newspaper reports called Maria a child virtuoso. She and Wolfgang wowed audiences in Munich, Vienna, Paris, London, the Hague, Germany, and Switzerland.

Musical collaborators and best friends, the Mozart children toured for more than three years, covering several thousand miles by horse-drawn carriage, stopping in eighty-eight cities and performing for many thousands of people.

Before Wolfgang could write, his big sister wrote down his compositions for him. In England, while their father was ill, Maria helped Wolfgang write his first symphony. We don't know if they composed music together—or if she ever wrote a symphony of her own.

When Wolfgang and his father left for Italy where Wolfgang learned to play more instruments and to improvise and compose, Maria was left behind. Scholars guess that the family didn't have enough money to bring both children on the tour. (Musicians had to take whatever payment was offered. Leopold Mozart once complained of having seven or eight gold watches and no money.) The musical education of a court composer and performer was also thought unnecessary and inappropriate for a young woman. (Organ playing, for instance, was thought unsuitable for women because you had to move your legs to push the pedals.) Only a handful of women at the time, mainly singers, were professional musicians.

Though Maria was a musical prodigy, unlike Wolfgang, she was not encouraged to read music on sight, vary a melody, change keys, play from a figured bass, or improvise. To her father's astonishment, she mastered all of these skills anyway. She even composed music and at least one noted musician, her brother Wolfgang, thought her compositions were brilliant. But we don't know what her pieces sounded like, for they have been lost forever.

When Wolfgang went on another tour a few years later with his mother, Maria wept bitterly. We don't know for sure what she wept for: the absence of her dear brother and mother, boredom, or musical frustration. Maria's mother died on this tour, in Paris.

While traveling without his sister, Wolfgang wrote her playful, teasing, loving letters. While at home between tours, he composed music—beautiful, challenging music—especially for her to play. In honor of Maria's twenty-fifth birthday, Wolfgang wrote the D Major Divertimento (K. 251). And over the course of his life, he dedicated many compositions, including a number of operas, to her.

In 1784, at age thirty-three, Maria married an aristocrat, Johann Baptist von Berchtold zu Sonnenburg, who had been widowed twice and already had five children. Maria moved to St. Gilgen, a tiny town six hours by carriage from Salzburg.

Her father gave her a fortepiano as a wedding present, but it went horribly out of tune soon after she moved to St. Gilgen. We can gather from letters from her father that it took more than two years for a tuner to make the trip.

Maria had three children of her own, one of whom died as an infant. In the course of her life, Maria taught many young musicians to play piano, including her stepchildren and children.

When Wolfgang died in 1791, at the age of thirty-five, Maria mourned the loss of her brother and cherished his memory. After moving back to Salzburg following the death of her husband, she went door-to-door, collecting copies of Wolfgang's compositions for publication.

When she was in her seventies, Maria went blind and lost the use of her left hand. But she continued to play her piano, the very instrument she and Wolfgang had played together as children. On October 29, 1829, at the age of seventy-eight, Maria died. Found on the piano were scores from her brother's operas *Don Giovanni* and *The Magic Flute*, probably the last music she ever played.

On their childhood tour, Wolfgang often played blindfolded to astonish audiences. At the end of her life, his sister Maria also played blind, and with only one hand, for the sheer love of music.

The Scores

Though Maria Anna's compositions have been lost, we can still listen to music that her brother Wolfgang wrote with her and especially *for* her on the CD *For Nannerl* performed by Wolfgang Brunner and Leonore von Stauss (Profil Medien GmbH, 2006).

The Orchestra

Many players have been instrumental in making this book possible. My sincere thanks to:

The Patron: Literary Arts and the Oregon Literary Fellowship, for breathing life and needed funds into the project when I discovered that the only biographies of Maria Anna Mozart were written in German.

The Strings: My husband, Craig, for setting me up with German-to-English translation software; Michelle Blair, Addie Kaye Boswell, Melissa Dalton, Noah Jenkins, and Lora Lyn Worden for essential research and translation assistance; and Michelle McCann and Nicole Schreiber for insightful feedback.

The Winds: Eva Rieger, Ph.D., professor of music history at the University of Bremen and author of the German-language biography *Nannerl Mozart: Leben einer Kunstlerin im 18 Jahrhundert (Nannerl Mozart: Life of an Artist in the 1800s)* for letting me run her book through translation software and for sharing insights by phone. Stan Stanford, Ph.D., professor of music at Portland State University and Genievière Geffray, a librarian at the Mozarteum in Salzburg, Austria, for answering countless questions.

The Brass: Abigail Samoun, my editor, for believing in me as a writer and an artist.

Bibliography

Books
Glover, Jane. *Mozart's Women: His Family, His Friends, His Music.* New York: HarperCollins, 2005.
Halliwell, Ruth. *The Mozart Family: Four Lives in Social Context.* Oxford: Clarendon Press, 1998.
Hummel, Walter. *Nannerl: Wolfgang Amadeus Mozarts Schwester. (Nannerl: Wolfgang Amadeus Mozart's Sister.)* Amalthea-Verlag, 1952.
Rieger, Eva. *Nannerl Mozart: Leben einer Kunstlerin im 18 Jahrhundert (Nannerl Mozart: Life of an Artist in the 1800s.)* Frankfurt: Insel, 1991 and 2005.
Sadie, Stanley. *Mozart: The Early Years 1756-1781.* New York: W. W. Norton, 2006.
Soloman, Maynard. *Mozart: A Life.* New York: HarperCollins, 1995

Letters and Documents
Anderson, Emily (ed.). *The Letters of Mozart and His Family, Volumes I and II.* New York: St. Martin's Press, 1966.
Deutsch, Otto Erich (ed.). *Mozart: A Documentary Biography.* Stanford: Stanford University Press, 1965.
Eisen, Cliff (ed.). *New Mozart Documents.* Stanford: Stanford University Press, 1991.
Mozart, Leopold. *Nannerl Notenbuch 1759.* Germany: Heinrichshofen's Verlag: 1969.
Novello, Mary and Vincent. *A Mozart Pilgrimage: Being the Travel Diaries of Vincent and Mary Novello in the Year 1829.* London: Ernst Eulenburg Ltd, 1975.

Personal Interviews
Geffray, Genievière, director of the library at the Mozarteum in Salzburg, Austria. Email interviews, summer and fall 2007.
Rieger, Eva, Ph.D., professor of music history at the University of Bremen. Phone and email interviews, summer and fall 2007.
Stanford, Stan, Ph.D., professor of music at Portland State University. Interview summer 2007.